MATH FUN

WITH TRICKY LINES AND SHAPES

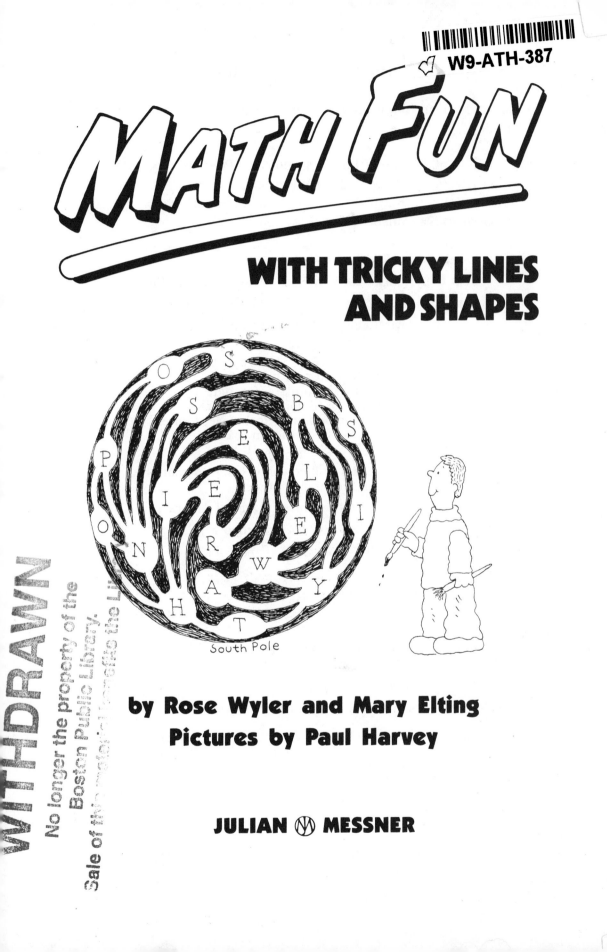

South Pole

by Rose Wyler and Mary Elting
Pictures by Paul Harvey

JULIAN Ⓜ MESSNER

Acknowledgments

For advice and helpful suggestions about this book the authors thank:

Rachel Folsom, coauthor of *MacIntosh Pascal*
Eva-Lee Baird, New York City Public Schools
Erica Voolich, Math Specialist to the Friends School,
    Cambridge, Massachusetts

Published by Julian Messner,
a division of Simon & Schuster,
Simon & Schuster Building, Rockefeller Center,
1230 Avenue of the Americas,
New York, New York 10020.

JULIAN MESSNER and colophon are trademarks
of Simon & Schuster.

Manufactured in the United States of America.

10 9 8 7 6 5 4 3 2 1 (hardcover)

10 9 8 7 6 5 4 3 2 1 (paperback)

Library of Congress Cataloging-in-Publication Data

Wyler, Rose.
    Math fun with tricky lines and shapes / by Rose Wyler
and Mary Elting; illustrations by Paul Harvey.
       p.   cm. — (Math fun)
    Includes index.
    Summary: Presents mathematical recreations exploring geometrical
concepts.
    1. Geometry—Juvenile literature.   [1. Mathematical
recreations.   2. Geometry.]   I. Elting, Mary.   II. Harvey, Paul,
ill.   III. Title.   IV. Series.
   QA445.5.W95 1992
   793.7'4—dc20
                              92-3513
                               CIP
                               AC

ISBN 0-671-74315-5 (library) ISBN 0-671-74316-3 (paper)

Hi!

Here are games and tricks and puzzles for you to explore. Some will point to the surprising places where math is at work in the world around you. Some will make you chuckle. You'll find a couple of mysteries, a few riddles, even some math magic you can stage to astonish your friends. So turn the pages and have fun.

Rose Wyler and Mary Elting

TABLE OF CONTENTS

SEEING THINGS 46

ZANY BUT BRAINY 52

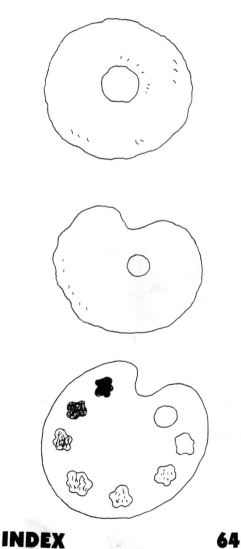

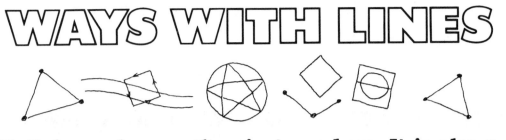

WAYS WITH LINES

Math is much more than just numbers. It is also a special way of looking at lines and shapes. Math helps you discover patterns and connections in angles and curves, circles and squares. There are even surprising math rules that you will find when you play games with shapes and lines.

YOUR VERY OWN LINES

Look at the lines in the palms of your hands. You'll never see any other palm lines like them. No one in the world has exactly the same line patterns that you have.

Do you find lines that are parallel—that is, that run in the same direction and are the same distance apart? Are some of them curved? Do some of these lines cross to form an X or an angle or some other shape? Are the patterns in both your palms the same?

Use a hand mirror to compare the soles of your feet, left and right. They, too, have lines and patterns. Do they match? Compare yours with the lines and patterns on your friends' feet.

Luckily, your sole lines are unlike anyone else's. If you were born in a hospital, a nurse probably pressed the sole of your foot against an ink pad, then pressed your foot on a special sheet of paper to make a sole print. The print would guarantee that you didn't get mixed up with any other baby when you went home. The hospital still has your sole print. You could even go and look at it. Your print is much bigger now, but the patterns the lines make are still the same.

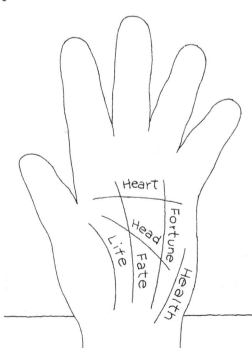

I foresee trouble with the decimal point.

FUTURE LINES?

Can the lines and patterns on the palms of your hands tell what your future is going to be? A fortune-teller may try to make you believe it. That kind of fortune-telling, called palmistry, began at least 2,500 years ago, and palmists in those days had to be very careful what they said. Suppose a palmist told a king that he might live a very long time. And suppose he died young. No problem. The palmist was careful to tell the king he *might* live to be old.

There has never been any scientific evidence that palm lines tell the future. But the lines are useful at times. The bumps and creases they form help you get a good grip on things you pick up.

Can You . . . ?

1. Can you draw two straight lines without lifting your pencil from the paper?

2. Can you draw two parallel lines that aren't straight?

3. Can you find a straight line that curves?

4. Can you find a line that goes around and around but never comes back to the same place?

Yes, You Can!

1. To draw two straight lines without lifting your pencil, draw an angle.

2. You can draw two parallel lines that are wavy, like this:

3. Look at a globe, and you'll see many straight lines that are curved. To test whether a straight line can be curved, take a piece of string and lay it from the north pole to the south pole on a globe. The string marks the shortest way to travel between the two poles. Because a straight line is the shortest distance between two points, the curving line on the globe is straight.

4. Look at a slinky toy, and you'll
   see a line that goes around and
   around but never comes back to
   the same place. This shape, in
   which every curving part fits
   over every other curving part, is
   called a helix. A helix is one
   kind of spiral. Another kind has
   curves that get wider as they go
   around a central point.

DOODLE SKATING

Kate's Star

Sonya's Star

Kate and Sonya were
ice-skating on a pond. "I
can make a star in a circle on the
ice without skating over any of
the lines twice," said Kate. And
she did.

"I can do something harder,"
Sonya said. "I can skate a
six-pointed star." And she did.

Can you draw Kate's
five-pointed star and Sonya's
six-pointed star without lifting
your pencil or tracing any line
twice?

Try the figure below, too.

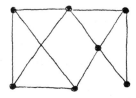

DOODLE GAMES

After Kate and Sonya went home, they doodled some more. You can play the same doodle games they played. All you need is a friend, plus paper and pencil.

Here are three figures. Each person playing the game should look at the first figure and then try to copy it exactly without lifting the pencil from the paper. The winner is the doodler who finishes first.

What is a line? The dictionary says it is a continuous mark. That means it could go on forever. Of course, a mark doesn't go on forever when you draw it on paper. You start it and stop it at places you choose. Mathematicians call that kind of mark a *line segment*. But since we are just having fun with lines, we're leaving off the word *segment.*

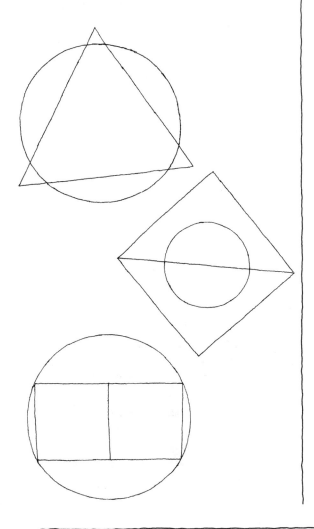

HOW TO BE A DOODLE CHAMP

The arrows on page 10 show you how to draw five of the figures on pages 8 and 9. But where is the little rectangular figure at the bottom of page 8? This was a sneaky trick. You can't draw it without lifting your pencil, no matter how many times you try. Don't be mad. This trick reveals a secret that will make you a winner if anyone ever tries to fool you again. Using math, you can tell ahead of time whether or not you can draw one continuous line without repeating any part of a figure.

Here's what you do: Examine every point where lines in the figure meet. If an even number of lines come together at all the points, you can draw the figure without lifting your pencil. That is, if two, four, or six lines come together, you're OK. But what if there are three lines meeting at any point? You are still OK if the figure has *just two* points where three lines (or any other odd number) meet. If a figure has more than two such odd meeting points, forget it. The rectangular figure has more than two points where three lines meet. That means your pencil will get stuck in a corner when you try it.

start

GRIDLOCK ALERT!

Traffic jams on a main street in a big city were getting worse and worse. Too many trucks, cars, and buses were clogging the traffic flow. But network math showed an astonishing thing: If *no* traffic was allowed on the main street, the traffic would move better on the other streets! Moreover, it showed how to create special routes for trucks and buses and how to change traffic rules to keep things moving better on all the city streets.

Leonard Euler went on to be a very great mathematician. He studied other problems in which connections between points, like the seven bridges, are important. This area of math is now called network theory.

THE PUZZLE THAT PEOPLE TRIED TO SOLVE WITH THEIR FEET

People who lived in the city of Königsberg long ago had a puzzle that they tried to solve with their feet as well as their heads. How could they find a route that would take them over every one of the city's seven bridges without crossing any bridge more than once?

Can you solve the puzzle, using your finger to do the walking? Try it and see.

If you can't find the answer, don't feel discouraged. The puzzle also bothered a bright young Swiss student named Leonard Euler. About 250 years ago, Euler experimented with a map of the bridges and finally decided the puzzle was unsolvable. But because he loved math, he decided to find a mathematical rule for this and similar problems.

Euler's rule became famous! If a figure has more than two points where an odd number of lines meet, it can't be traced without crossing some point twice.

P.S. Compare the bridges of Königsberg with the rectangular figure on page 8.

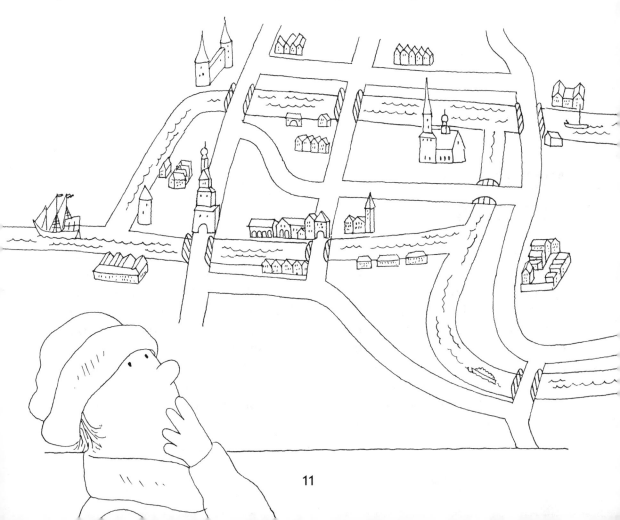

11

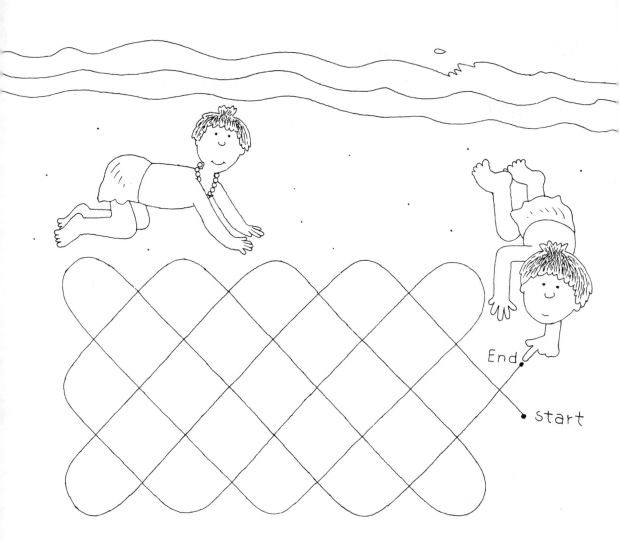

End

start

PUZZLE IN THE SAND

Children who live on a group of islands called Vanuatu in the Pacific Ocean often play this tracing game. Beginning at the place labeled *Start* and ending at *End*, a child uses a finger to draw a design in the sand. The child traces a continuous line and never travels along a line already drawn. Know how it's done? See the drawing on page 14.

To some people, figures like the puzzles in the sand aren't just games. Like the seven-bridge puzzle, they are called *networks*. There are serious network problems to be solved every day all over the world. For example, network math helps people plan where to put electric wires in new buildings. It also helps plan ways to switch millions of telephone calls so that callers don't get the wrong number.

LINE THEM UP

Here are some connection games for you and a friend. You'll need graph paper to work them out. Before you start, copy on your graph paper the arrangements of the dots shown on the diagram. Make one copy for yourself and one for your partner. When that's done, both of you read the rules:

Using only five straight lines, you must pass your pencil through all twelve dots. You must touch one dot at the start of the game and a different dot at the end, and you can't lift your pencil from the paper. The lines may cross. Each line must go through at least two dots and can't go through the same dot twice.

Ready? Go! See who can solve the puzzle first.

Hint: You can start or end *outside* the square.

On page 14 you will find some of the ways to solve the puzzle. There are others that you may discover, but the player who first gets nine of them is the winner.

Riddle: What's in a line but not in a circle? Turn the page to find out.

Answer to Puzzle in the Sand

To solve the network puzzle, let your finger follow the letters of the alphabet as you draw the continuous lines. That's just the way the kids in Vanuatu play the game.

Is this how you did it?

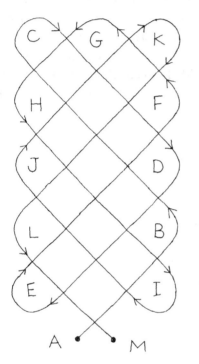

Answer to Line Them Up

The first nine solutions to the dot puzzle are the easy ones. For more fun, glance quickly at the three fancy figures. They will give you a general idea of more ways to solve the puzzle. Then try some other fancy solutions.

Answer to Riddle: the letter *n*

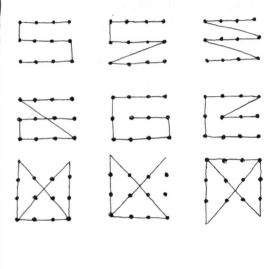

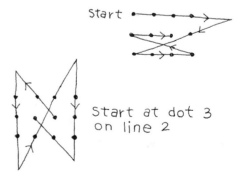

NO LEFT TURNS

Somebody borrowed Greg's bicycle and returned it with a damaged handlebar. Greg could still ride straight ahead and turn to the right, but the bike wouldn't go to the left. It had to be fixed. So Greg started riding to the repair shop. And that was easier said than done because of the pesky right-turn-only handlebar.

Look at the map of Greg's town. Then plan a route he could take to the bike shop by going only straight ahead or to the right. Can you get him there?

You'll find Greg's route on the next page.

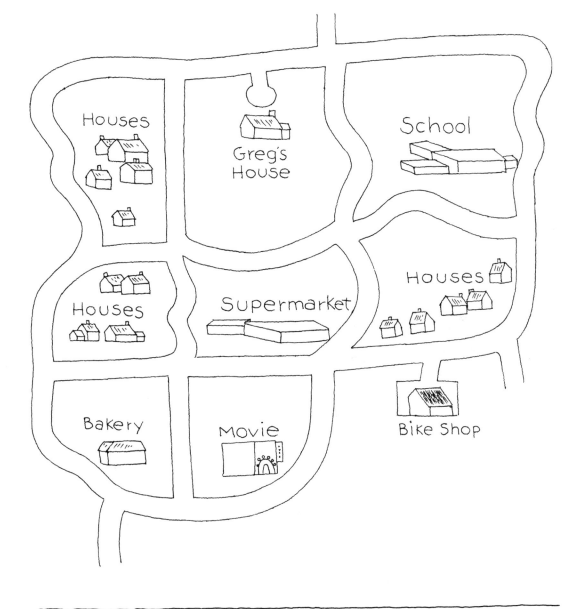

Another scientist put street lights on a little maze in a darkened room. He wanted to learn whether a rat could run the maze in the dark after it had learned its way on lighted paths. Sure enough, even with the lights off, the rat had no problem. Its other senses helped it remember where to go.

Other animals have passed the maze test, too. A cat, a raccoon, mice, ants, even worms can all learn the winding ways to food. Animals learn by trying, making mistakes, and trying again. People can also use their ability to think ahead. Can you think of a good way to get into and out of a maze?

MYSTERY MAZE

One day some young people were hiking in the stony mountains in southern California. A rainstorm had recently washed the earth away from a large rock near their trail. There the hikers saw something that looked like a page from a huge puzzle book carved into the rock's hard face. They knew that it was a maze. But who had carved it, and why?

There are many other mystery mazes that have been found on rocks in California. Scientists believe that Native Americans made the carvings when they lived there hundreds of years ago. No stories or legends exist about the reasons for carving the mazes. A scientist who has studied them says they may have some religious meaning. Perhaps ancient ceremonies were performed around the rocks. The mystery mazes will probably always be just that, a mystery. You can at least trace this one with your finger and solve the puzzle of how to get to the center and back out.

ROUND, SQUARE AND POINTED

A line can form a circle or a square or a triangle and a lot of other shapes, too. When a shape has length and width but not thickness, we call it two-dimensional. It is flat, like the puzzle on this page.

OOPS!

A man named Sam Lloyd, probably the world's greatest creator of puzzles, made up his first one when he was a teenager. His family had thought he would grow up to be an engineer, but he got too interested in magic tricks, ventriloquism, chess, and puzzles. A puzzle he called "The Canals of Mars" told the reader to spell a complete sentence by tracing a path from one letter to another. The path should start at the South Pole and should use each letter only once. When he published the puzzle in a magazine, fifty thousand people sent him the right answer: "There is no possible way."

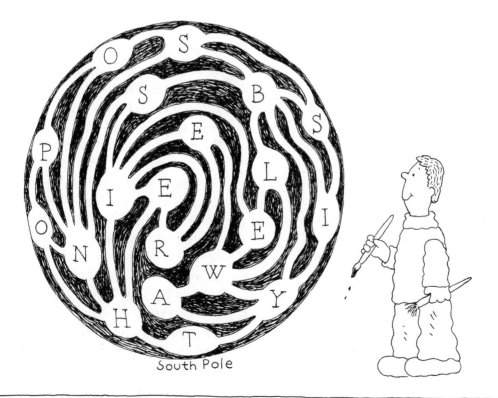

South Pole

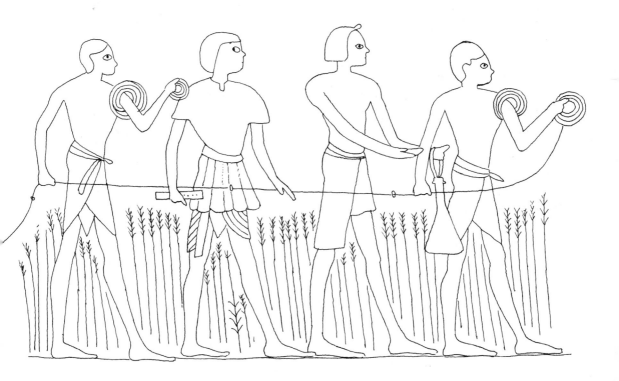

FROM ROPE TO RULERS

People began to study squares and triangles and other shapes a very long time ago. In ancient Egypt farmers needed to know the shapes and sizes of their grain fields. Why? Because every year the Nile River flooded its banks and washed away boundary markers around fields.

After each flood, men called "rope stretchers" came to put the markers back. Their ropes had knots that showed measures, the way a ruler shows inches or centimeters. Two or three of the "stretchers" would pull the rope tight and put markers in the ground where the knots showed they should be placed. Now the farmers could see where to plant their fields again. An Egyptian artist painted the men and their ropes 3,400 years ago.

Many years later people in Greece invented a way to use math for measuring shapes. It is from them that we get our word for the study of shapes— *geometry*. It combines two Greek words that mean to measure the earth.

SECRET OF THE PENTAGRAM

A famous ancient Greek math teacher was Pythagoras. His students loved to talk about the wonderful things you could do with numbers and shapes, and they formed a sort of secret math club.

The club members thought that one special figure called a pentagram was magical. To make it they drew a five-pointed star inside a pentagon. The pentagram could bring you good luck and keep you healthy, they said.

You can make a pentagram from a long, narrow strip of white tissue paper—the kind used to wrap gifts. Tie the strip into the kind of knot shown in the diagram, pull it snug, and press the knot flat to form a pentagon. Hold it up to the light, and you will see a shadowy five-pointed star.

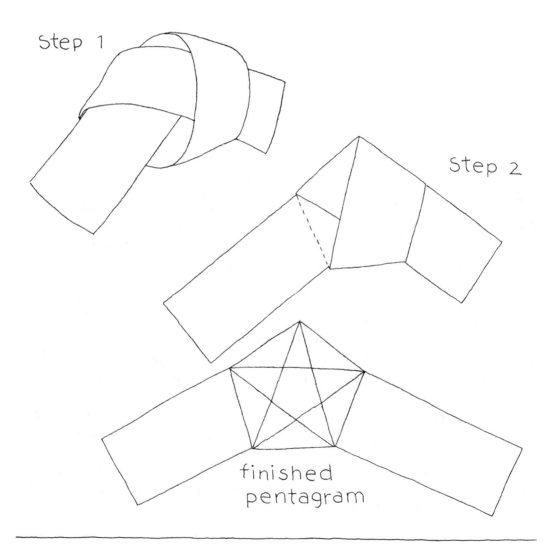

Step 1

Step 2

finished
pentagram

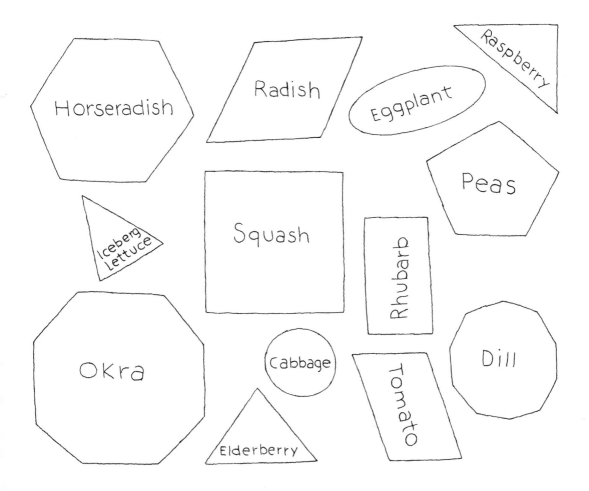

GEOMETRIC GARDEN

Becky's grandfather has a garden where he raises many different vegetables and fruits. He plants each kind in a patch of land shaped in a special way. The shapes he has chosen all have geometric names. And each plant has a name that begins with the same letter as the name of the patch where it will grow. For example, cabbage will be planted in a circle.

Here are the names of his plants: horseradish, pea, elderberry, radish, raspberry, squash, tomato, rhubarb, cabbage, dill, okra, eggplant, iceberg lettuce. In which patch will each be planted? See if you can dig up the answers. Then look on the next page.

These are the shapes in
Grandpa's garden

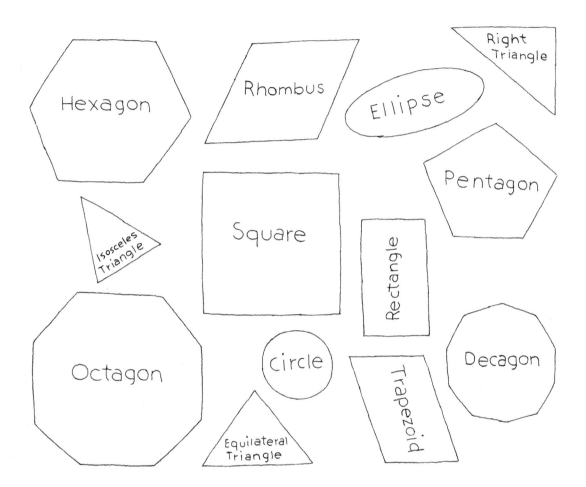

Are there any other two-dimensional shapes? There are actually just as many as you want to draw. Besides the thirteen in Grandpa's garden, you can discover in math books other shapes with special names. Some of them are: heptagon (seven-sided), nonagon (nine-sided), dodecagon (twelve-sided), trapezium (a four-sided shape with no parallel sides).

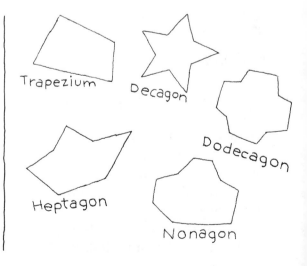

CRACKING THE CODE

The boys in Sonya's class were standing in one corner of the room, laughing and whispering and acting mysterious.

"They're up to something," Sonya said to her friend Kate.

"I'll find out," Kate said. "I'll ask Jack."

Jack was Kate's twin brother, who usually told her everything. But this time all he said was "We're starting the GNA club."

"What's that?" Kate asked.

"If you have to know, it stands for Girls Not Allowed," Jack answered.

"That's not fair!" said Kate.

Sonya agreed with her. "Well," she said, "maybe we can get them to change their minds. If we want them to, that is."

The boys went on acting important. They whispered in little groups and got together in the classroom after school.

That evening, when Kate and Jack were doing homework at the dining room table, Kate noticed that her brother was drawing something. But he kept his hand around the paper, as if he didn't want her to see it.

"It's club stuff," Kate said to herself. "I just know it is."

Jack finished his homework; then he crumpled up the sheet of paper, tossed it in the wastebasket, and went out to ride his bike.

Kate stared at the wastebasket. Should she take out the crumpled wad and peek? "It's not fair to peek," she thought. "But GNA isn't fair, either." Suddenly she made up her mind. Fair or not, she snatched out the wad and put it in her bookbag.

This is what Kate showed Sonya the next morning:

"It has to mean something," said Kate. "The way Jack acted I know it's a secret of some kind."

"Let's think," Sonya said.

The girls looked and looked at the drawings. "Do you suppose it could be a code?" Kate said.

"A code! Of course! I've got it!" Sonya began to write on the scrap of paper. "See—that's it!"

Can you figure out the word that Jack's drawings spelled in code? Look back at the names of the shapes on page 24, then read on.

"Look at the first letters in the names of the shapes," said Sonya. "They spell CONTACT. But what could that mean?"

"I bet it's the password for that old club of theirs," Kate said. "So what?"

"Let's try it and see," said Sonya.

The next time they saw the boys going into the classroom after school, Sonya and Kate sneaked up to the closed door and knocked. When the door opened a crack, Sonya whispered, "Contact!"

The door opened wide. And then there was a big rumpus. But after a while the boys agreed that if Sonya and Kate were smart enough to break the code, they could be members of the club.

"Not just us," Kate said. "You have to be fair. If all the boys in our class can belong, you should let all the girls belong. If they want to, that is."

There was some more discussion, but the boys finally agreed.

"One more thing," Sonya said. "We have to change the name. No more GNA." But they couldn't agree on a name.

What do you think they should call their club?

27

SEVEN CLEVER PIECES

Before the days of television, families often did puzzles together after dinner. Maybe your great-great-grandmother had a set of seven little blocks called tangram, or Chinese puzzle. The blocks could be arranged to make figures that looked like people or animals or things such as boats. Great-great-granny might have made dressed-up tangram ladies wearing big skirts. Now you can make your own tangram figures.

Copy the diagram on page 29 onto a piece of paper, and cut it up. Try putting together a woman with a pack on her back. What other figures and designs can you create?

People once thought the Chinese invented the tangram game and named it for a god called Tan. But the Chinese never heard of such a god! Probably the puzzle's original name was *Chi-Chiao*, which means "seven clever pieces." Who brought it here from China and changed its name? What does *tangram* mean? No one really knows.

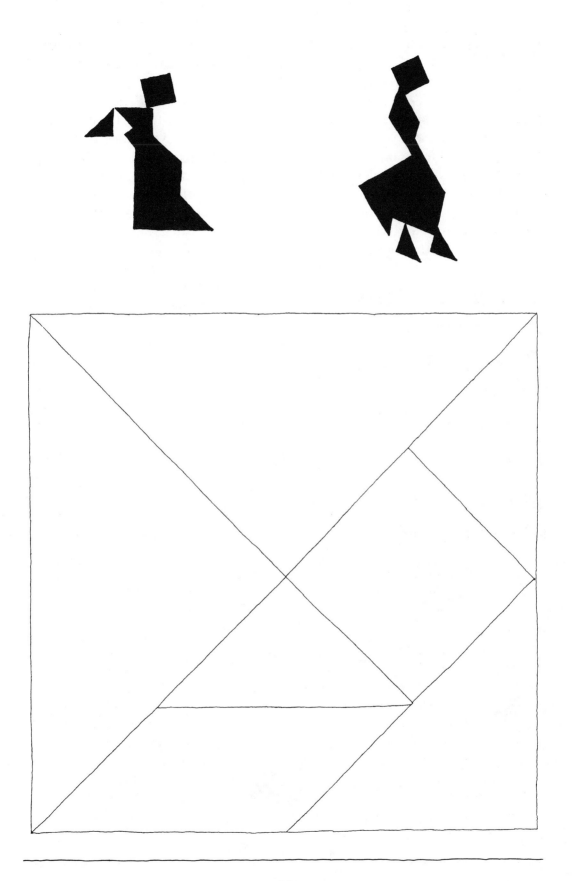

QUICKIE

Play this game with two friends. First, cut out three sets of tangram shapes, one for each of you. "Now," you say, "let's put the pieces back together into the original square and see who does it first." It's harder than you might think, because that's not what you usually do with the pieces.

THE DOUGHNUT AND THE DINOSAUR

Can you cut apart a doughnut and turn it into a snake? This is an old-time puzzle.

The next one is more modern. Storytellers invented dragons that ate people. Dinosaurs look almost as if someone had invented them, but they really existed. Can you trace this imaginary dragon, cut it apart, and then put the pieces back together in the shape of a real plant-eating dinosaur named *Camarasaurus*?

Hint: Wings made dragons special. What was special about the plant-eaters?

SUPER PUZZLES

The scientists who study dinosaurs are called paleontologists. When they found the skeleton of a *Camarasaurus* buried in the earth, its bones were mixed up with the bones of several other kinds of dinosaurs. They had all been washed away together in a flood after they died 140 million years ago. The bone pile was a super puzzle that paleontologists had to solve. Which foot bones went with which leg bones? Which head belonged on *Camarasaurus*'s neck?

The wonderful thing about being a paleontologist is that the puzzles never seem to end. Every year someone discovers and digs up the bones of a new dinosaur. Sometimes it is a brand-new kind. Once some scientists were digging where they expected to find small skeletons. Instead they uncovered one piece of a backbone they could hardly believe. It was about six feet (two meters) long and more than three feet (one meter) wide. This creature must have been more than a hundred feet (thirty-five meters) long when it was alive. That's as long as three school buses. Imagine putting together a puzzle with parts that size!

Camarasaurus was up to sixty-five feet (twenty meters) long. Perhaps it used its heavy tail to whack any meat-eater that attacked it.

MRS. MURDOCK'S FLOOR

Mrs. Murdock was having a new tile floor put in her kitchen. She wanted all the tiles to be the same shape, with no spaces between them.

"Here are some shapes that will work," said the tile man who had come to do the job. He showed her a page from his sample book.

"Hmm," said Mrs. Murdock. "I can see how the rectangles fit, side by side and row by row. The triangles fit, too. You just turn half of them upside down. The hexagons aren't hard, either." She drew the patterns.

But then she noticed a fourth shape that looked like this:

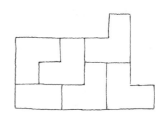

"I don't think it works," she said.

"It really does," the tile man answered. "But I always get mixed up unless I look at the instructions in the sample book." He showed her the page.

"Beautiful!" she said. "That's the one I want."

Can you find another way to fit the tiles together?

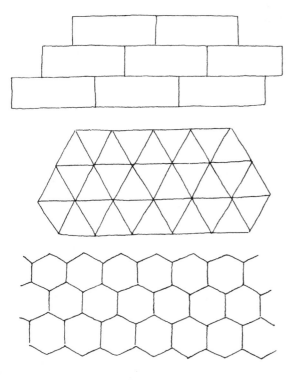

What would Mrs. Murdock's floor look like if she had insisted on having pentagon-shaped tiles? Very peculiar! There is a math rule about fitting together tiles in the shape of pentagons and other regular straight-sided shapes: Where the angles in these tiling shapes come together, they must always fill a complete circle.

Why Mrs. Murdock could not have pentagon-shaped tiles:

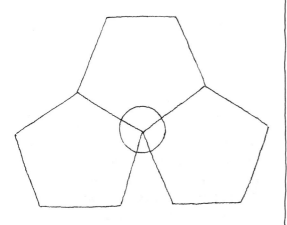

YOUR OWN PATTERNS

Another word for tiling is tessellation. Long ago tessellation meant using little colored tiles to make patterns in floors and on walls. People who wove cloth also used patterns with colored threads, and they had to plan which color was woven over and which was woven under.

In cloth factories now, weavers use math to form tessellated patterns. Mathematicians like to experiment with the kinds of rules they use. Artists experiment with them, too, and they create fancy ones for fun and to decorate such things as wallpaper and dishes.

You can make paper tessellations with your own drawings. Start with a rectangle. Snip a shape from the right side and paste it on the left side. Use this as a pattern, and cut out as many as you want to fit together.

PI FOR PUPS

Roy lives next door to a man whose big dog had ten puppies! When the pups were small, the square pen where they lived with their mother was large enough. But as they grew, the pen got more and more crowded.

"Why don't you make them a bigger one?" Roy asked.

"I don't have any more fencing to put around a larger pen," the man answered.

"I can show you how to use this same fence and still give the pups more room to play," Roy said. "You just have to change the shape of the pen."

The neighbor took Roy's advice.

Roy knows an interesting math secret: If a circle and a square are the same distance around, the circle encloses more space. Here's another way of saying the same thing: If the circumference of a circle (the distance around it) and the perimeter (the distance around it) of a square are the same, the area within the circle is larger.

How much larger was the new pen?

First, Roy measured the perimeter of the square pen. It was 11 feet on each side; so 11 × 4 = 44 feet. Because the same fence enclosed the circular pen, the circumference of that pen was also 44 feet.

Now it's easy to find out how much space there was inside the square. Roy knows, as you probably do, that you just multiply the length by the width. That is, 11 × 11 = 121 square feet. That was the area of the square. If you want to prove it, draw a figure 11 squares long and 11 squares wide on graph paper, and count the number of squares inside.

But what is the secret of the circle's area?

To find the area of the new pen, Roy had to do more math, using a special number called *pi* (pronounced "pie"). It is a strange number. It isn't even an exact number! It is somewhere between $3\frac{1}{7}$ and $3\frac{10}{71}$. To make things simple, Roy decided on $3\frac{1}{7}$. Now he used three rules about circles.

1. **To find the distance across a circle (its diameter), you divide its circumference by pi.**

2. **To find the radius (the distance from the center to the circumference), you divide the diameter in half.**

3. **To find the area of a circle, you multiply the radius by itself and then multiply by pi.**

Roy's calculation told him the area of the circle was 154 square feet.

How much larger was the puppies' new pen? Subtract the area of the square from the area of the circle: $154 - 121 = 33$ square feet!

When Roy used $3\frac{1}{7}$ for pi, he didn't get the exact area of the round pen. But it was close enough for the pups.

CATCHING UP WITH PI

In math books pi is always written with this symbol, π, which is the Greek letter p. Mathematicians in Europe started using the symbol almost two hundred years ago. But people knew about this peculiar number several thousand years before that. At first they simply figured it was exactly 3.

Later, mathematicians began to make more accurate measurements, and they discovered that the number for pi had to be a little larger than 3. Still later, they began using a decimal fraction instead of the ordinary fraction $3\frac{1}{7}$. Now pi was equal to 3.1418. Still more accurate calculations showed that the number should be 3.14159265. Even that was not completely accurate. Actually, the numbers on the right side of the decimal point could go on and on forever.

After computers were invented, it became a sort of game to add more numbers to pi. Finally a computer expert announced he had calculated it to two billion decimal places!

When you do pi problems, you will probably use 3.1416. Here is a way to remember the decimal places:

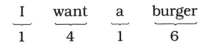

I	want	a	burger
1	4	1	6

FROM MARBLES TO HOT DOGS

How old were you when you first realized that two popsicles and two socks both had something to do with the number two? Probably you were in kindergarten. How long do you think it took your ancestors to figure that out? Two or three thousand years. But before people learned to use numbers, they were already doing math! The first math we know about started in Asia, and it was done with little objects made of baked clay.

MYSTERY MATH

Suppose you were a scientist exploring an ancient ruined town in Mesopotamia, in west Asia. One day you found a lot of little objects that looked like pyramids and marbles and tiny jars, all made of clay. Would you guess they were a child's playthings, maybe pieces for a game? That was what scientists once thought. Then a teacher at the University of Texas solved the mystery.

The people who made the "toys" were some of the first farmers—and mathematicians—in the world. To keep grain for

winter, a big community storehouse was built. After a while an argument must have started. How much wheat had one family contributed? Somehow, about ten thousand years ago, people worked out a system for keeping track of what they stored away, and the system lasted for hundreds and hundreds of years.

The ancient system worked like this: Somebody began to stay at the big storehouse to check in the baskets of grain that farmers brought. For every basketful a farmer received a marble-shaped ball of baked clay. Scientists call these objects *tokens.* For every big jar of oil, the farmer received a token shaped like a tiny oil jar.

After a while somebody invented the first piggy bank! It was a hollow ball of clay made to hold tokens. While the outside of the clay ball was still soft, it was marked. A mark left by a "marble" pressed into the wet clay meant that the farmer had delivered one basket of grain. Three round marble marks and one jar-shaped mark stood for three baskets of grain and one jar of oil. Tokens shaped like pyramids or eggs stood for other things. With the tokens inside, the piggy bank was baked. Now each farmer had an exact record of what he had put away. But if anyone questioned the marks on the outside, the farmer could break the ball carefully, and the tokens would prove he was right.

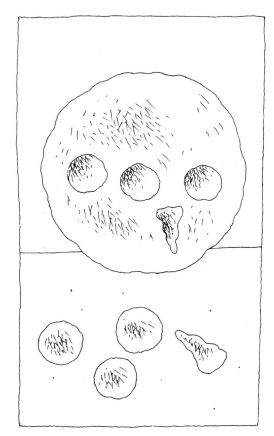

The first piggy bank

FROM SHAPES TO NUMBERS

The piggy banks full of tokens were used for a long, long time, until math with numbers was invented. Later, those solid token shapes interested mathematicians. Could they work out rules about pyramids and cubes and spheres? They could and did. One rule they discovered was this: There are a great many solid shapes, but only five of these shapes form a special group. Each solid shape in the group has several flat faces, and all its faces have the same size and shape.

Here are the five regular solid shapes and their names. If you're wondering why you don't find among them a sphere or a cylinder or a cone, remember the rule: The faces have to be flat. The sphere, cylinder, and cone all have curved surfaces.

You could mold all of the five solid shapes in clay, but there is an easier way to have fun with them. Try making paper shells of solid shapes by tracing and cutting and folding.

THE WICKED CUBE GAME

On page 39 are patterns for paper cubes that you will need for this game. On a piece of paper, copy the design in each square exactly. Then cut and fold on the dotted lines. Tuck in the rounded tabs. That's it.

Persuade a friend to make a set of the cubes, too. Now you both are ready to play the game, which has one simple rule: Stack your cubes in such a way that each side of the stack shows only one of the designs.

Get ready for a game that will haunt you. The winner is the one who first solves the secret of the wicked cubes. It *can* be done!

Suggestion: After you have learned the secret, don't take the cubes apart right away. First, make a note of the order in which you stacked them, so you can show off your skill some time later.

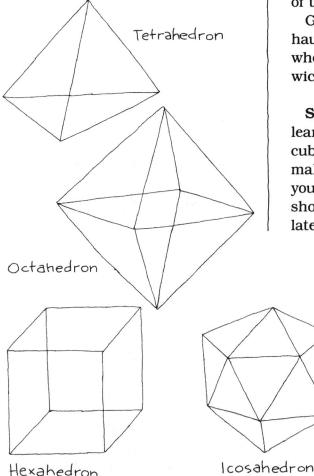

Tetrahedron

Octahedron

Hexahedron

Icosahedron

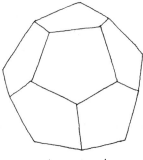

Dodecahedron

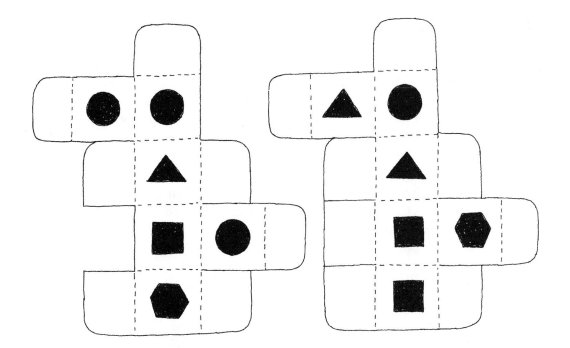

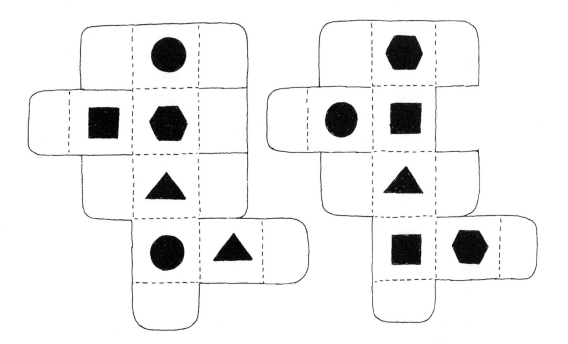

RECYCLING THE CUBES

At last! You have stacked your cubes. Maybe it's time to recycle them. Carefully unfold them, flatten them out, and cut them into separate squares. Next, cut some light cardboard into rectangles the size and shape of playing cards. On each of the cards, paste one of the cutout sides of a cube. Now you'll have a set of twenty-four playing cards.

(Get your friend to do the same thing, and you'll have a pack of forty-eight—perfect for a game of rummy or Old Maid.)

ASK A PYRAMID

A pyramid is a shape that fascinated the rulers of Egypt long ago. Why? Nobody knows for sure. Perhaps someone said there was magic in a pyramid. Some people still believe in pyramid magic, but there is no scientific evidence that the shape has any such mysterious power.

The Egyptian ruler Cheops decided to have an enormous pyramid, 492 feet (almost 150 meters) high—as tall as a skyscraper—built from huge blocks of stone.

What would you do if you were a ruler and wanted a pyramid like that? You would have to be sure that your builders knew math. The builders of ancient Egypt certainly did. They measured and figured out just where to put the blocks of stone so that the triangular sides of the pyramid met exactly at the top. We don't know who those math experts were or how they did their calculations, but the pyramids were built, and they are still standing today, almost five thousand years later.

You can build a pyramid of your own from modeling clay. But you can have much more fun with a special riddle pyramid made of paper. It will be easy if you copy the diagram on page 41 onto graph paper. Then follow these instructions:

Write the riddles on the triangles numbered 1, 2, and 3, and write the answers on triangle 4. After you cut out the pattern, crease the triangles and tabs along the dotted lines, and then fold. Paste side A to the tab labeled B, side C to the tab labeled D, and tab E will easily come all the way around to be pasted to side F.

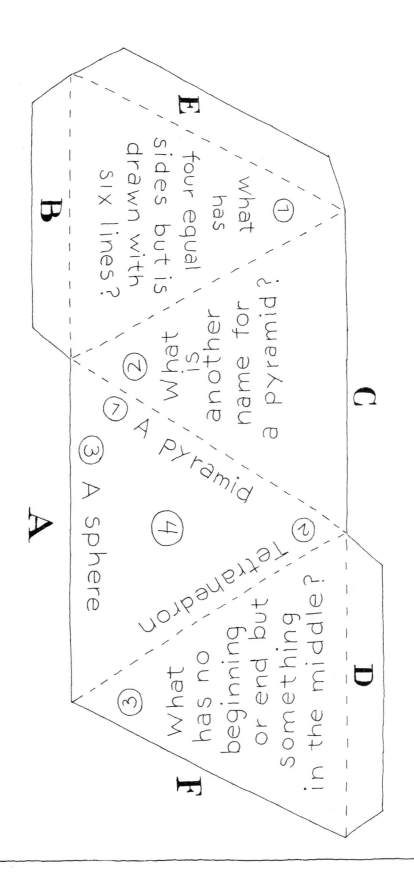

E

① what has another name for a pyramid?

four equal sides but is drawn with six lines?

B

② What is

① A Pyramid

③ A Sphere

A

C

④

② Tetrahedron

D

③ What has no beginning or end but say something in the middle?

F

NEW RIDDLE FOR THE SPHINX

Close to one big pyramid in Egypt is an enormous statue. It has been damaged and worn away in places, but it still looks like the body of a lion with a human head. Its name is the Sphinx.

An ancient legend said that the sphinx was a ferocious monster who destroyed people. Everyone who passed by it had to answer a riddle. Those who failed were destroyed. This is the famous riddle of the sphinx:

What walks on four legs in the morning, on two legs at noon, and on three legs at dusk?

And how about this new one for the Sphinx: What has four sides and no roof but isn't open on top? You won't be doomed even if you have to look for the answers on page 44.

SOME ODD ONES

Y ou can stack several little tetrahedrons together and make one big pyramid shape. Two pyramids fitted together make an octahedron. Stack four cubes, and you have a big cube shape. Or lay cubes side by side to make a shape called a prism. There are lots of different prisms. They all have sides that are flat but are not the same shape at the ends.

SWEET SHAPE

T here's one kind of prism you can eat! Bees make it by the thousands and store honey inside.

To form their honeycombs bees first make wax in their own bodies. Then they shape the wax into little hexagons that form the bottom of the honeycomb. Next they build up rectangles of wax on each of the hexagons' six edges, creating little six-sided wax cells. After filling these containers with honey, they make lids for the comb from more hexagons of wax. Each little honey-filled cell is an edible prism.

Can you think of other solid shapes that are good to eat? What about spheres?

You can make some sweet ones yourself. Freeze juice in ice-cube pans. Make a batch of gelatin dessert using less water than usual, and cut it into all kinds of prisms.

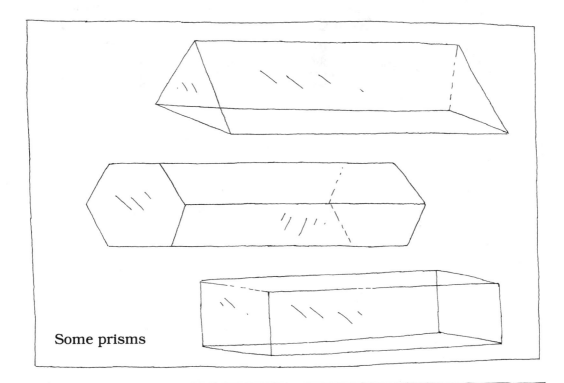

Some prisms

FAIR SHARE

Suppose you and twenty-four other kids are going on a picnic and you have to bring the hot dogs. You must buy enough so that each of you has two. The box you have is just wide enough to fit nine hot dogs in a row. You lay them in and discover that the box will hold only five rows of nine each. That's only forty-five hot dogs—not enough to go around twice. Some kids won't get a fair share.

Without bringing a bigger box or two boxes, what can you do?

The first picture shows hot dogs packed nine across, one above the other, in five rows. The second picture shows them packed nine across, then eight across, and so on in six rows. By reducing the space between them, you can fit in an extra row. Now you will have fifty-one hot dogs in the box—two apiece for twenty-five kids and an extra one for you because you know your math.

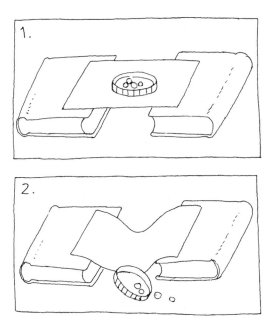

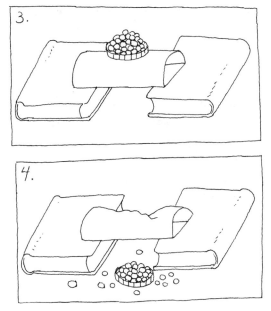

STRONG AS AN EGG

W hat? Strong as an ox, maybe, but is an egg really strong? The shell is, because of its shape. Try to break an egg by setting it on end on a plate and pushing downward on it. You'll see how strong that curving shape is.

People who built bridges discovered long ago that a curved shape under a road that crossed a river could hold up heavier-weight loads than a straight surface. Here's a way you can test that idea:

1. **Get two books, a card, a jar lid, and some small pebbles. Make the card into a bridge between the books. Now lay the jar lid on the bridge and put pebbles in it a few at a time.**

2. **When the bridge falls down, count the pebbles.**

3. **Now bend the card into a curved shape, prop it between the two books, and set the lid on top. Put pebbles into the lid till the card starts to collapse.**

4. **Count the pebbles. You'll see that the curved card can hold up a heavier load than the flat card.**

A curved shape called an *arch* and other curved shapes can be used to make buildings strong. One structure that is curved in all directions, like the end of an egg, is a dome. Dome-shaped roofs for buildings are so strong that they can be much wider than flat roofs.

SEEING THINGS

**"You can't fool me. I always know what I see."
Don't believe that for a minute. The best eyes in
the world can be fooled by tricky lines and shapes
that mathematicians call optical illusions. See if
your eyes are tricked in the next story and the
teasers that follow.**

FISH TALE

Long ago a wise woman who was making a journey came to a deep river that had to be crossed by boat. The two boatmen paid no attention to her. They were too busy arguing. They had been fishing, and each claimed his biggest fish was bigger than the other's biggest.

For a while the wise woman waited patiently. Then she stepped in between the boatmen and said, "Listen! If I can prove to you which fish is the larger, will you stop squabbling and take me across the river in your boat?"

The men agreed. So the wise woman put a mark like an O on the left side of one man's biggest fish and a mark like an X on the left side of the other man's biggest fish.

"Wait here," she told the boatmen, and carrying the fish,

she went down to a flat, sandy place on the riverbank. There she laid the fish on the sand and drew two figures around them.

Now the wise woman was ready, and she called the boatman whose fish was marked with an O. "Which fish is bigger?" she asked.

"Mine, of course," replied the boatman.

"Very well," said the wise woman. "You are satisfied. You have promised to stop quarreling. So you will not say another word to your partner and will take me across the river."

The boatman agreed, and the wise woman called the other man. While he was coming, she quickly switched the fish so that the one marked O now lay where the one marked X had been.

"Which is larger?" she asked.

"Mine, of course," replied the second boatman.

"Very well," said the wise woman. "You are satisfied. You have promised to stop quarreling. So you will not say another word to your partner and will take me across the river."

He agreed. With a secret smile, each of the boatmen put his fish into his bag, and together they rowed the wise woman across.

What was the wise woman's secret? She had seen that the boatmen's two fish were really the same size, and she knew that people's eyes often can be tricked. So she drew the two sets of lines in the sand and fooled each boatman in turn. Measure the fish, and you'll discover that your eyes, too, were mistaken.

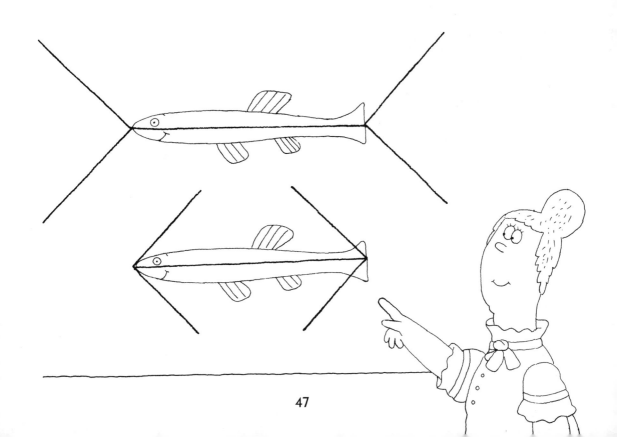

TRICKY SLINKY

Which way is this slinky facing? The drawing seems to change because your eyes shift the tiniest bit from one end to the other. They see the picture first one way, then the other, and your brain can't decide which way is right. Don't worry. Both are right.

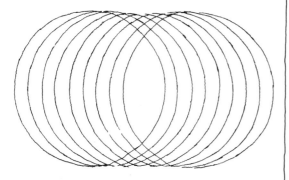

THE STRIPED SKIRT PROBLEM

Suppose a factory that made cloth decided to plan a new pattern. Somebody worked out the math for weaving black threads over and under the white threads in a very unusual way. Some of the new cloth was made into skirts. But when girls tried them on in a store, they all said, "Something is wrong. No matter how you pull to straighten the stripes they don't look parallel."

But the people at the factory said, "Measure the cloth for yourself. The lines in the pattern are perfectly parallel."

Do you believe that? Try measuring. The stripes are, in fact, the same distance apart. Their irregularity is an optical illusion. Still, you can't blame the girls for not liking the skirts.

The company that made that weird cloth was stubborn. They didn't want to throw it all away. The person who invented the design turned a piece of it this way and that and suddenly said, "Hey! I've got it! I know where we can sell all this stuff!" Can you guess what the idea was?

Try this: Lay the book flat on the table, then turn it slowly counterclockwise, and watch the pattern. The stripes will slowly begin to look parallel. So the cloth company sold the material to people who cut it, turned it just right, and made it into fancy car-seat covers.

THE GREAT PIE MYSTERY

Sherlock Holmes's friend Dr. Watson had a terrible cold. He couldn't talk, even in a whisper. So when the cook asked if he would like something to eat, he drew this picture and handed it to her:

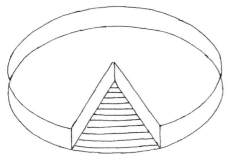

The cook looked at it. "I should say not!" she said. "I really didn't think you were so greedy."

Dr. Watson was puzzled. What was greedy about showing that he wanted her to cut him a piece of pie? When Holmes came in a few minutes later, the doctor handed him a note saying what had happened.

Holmes looked at the picture Dr. Watson had drawn. Then he laughed and asked the cook to come back. He handed her the drawing and said, "Is this what my friend asked for?"

She shook her head. "No, indeed," she said crossly. "What he wanted was almost a whole pie for himself, leaving just one piece for you. Don't you think that's very greedy?"

"It depends on how you look at things," Holmes answered. He took the drawing from her, turned it around, then handed it back. "Look at it again, please."

"Why, it's magic!" she said.

"Not magic. Just a simple illusion," Holmes said.

To see what Holmes meant, turn the book halfway around and look at Dr. Watson's drawing again. The change in what you seem to see is startling. A pie with one piece cut out has become an almost empty pie pan, with only one piece left in it! Next, bring the book back to the usual position, and now there's only one piece missing. Dr. Watson should have been more careful how he handed his picture to the cook.

You can find one more illusion in this drawing. Look at the picture for a few extra seconds. Can you see a triangular block standing upright in a hoop?

DOUBLE TRICK

Which of the kids standing in line is the tallest? Guess before you measure.

The artist has tricked you with an optical illusion. Actually, you have been tricked by two illusions:

1. **The artist has followed a mathematical rule for drawing a room that *looks* real. In a real cafeteria all the tiles on the floor and ceiling would be the** same size, but to make them appear to be the same size the artist had to draw them smaller and smaller all the way across the page. The rule is: The farther away things are from your eyes, the smaller they look.

2. **The artist didn't follow this rule when drawing the kids standing in line. By making them all the same size, the artist created the illusion that the most distant was the biggest. So this picture is a double trick.**

WEIRD ROAD, WACKY ANGLE

Because our eyes fool us, we need math to measure and explain what we see. Artists in Europe discovered this about six hundred years ago. Before that they drew everything the way you probably did in kindergarten. To show a cow in the distance, you drew it at the top of the page. That is what ancient artists did.

When artists began to get interested in science and math, they discovered what they called *perspective*—math rules to make their pictures look real. They began to pay attention to the weird thing that happens when you look down a long road. You know that the sides of the road are parallel, but the space between the sides seems to get narrower in the distance. At the horizon the sides seem to meet. This is called the vanishing point. If you want to sketch this illusion, a person far down the road has to be drawn smaller in order to fit into the narrower space.

In a real room the floor and the wall meet at right angles. But to make them look real in a picture, the artist has to draw them meeting at a different angle. The more artists learned about the math of angles, the more real their pictures became. Many artists today follow the rules of perspective, even though they don't do precise measuring.

TRICKING THE FISH AND THE KITTEN

Scientists believe that animals, like people, are sometimes fooled by what they see. Some birds have white undersides that may trick the fish they eat. To the fish, a gull or pelican may seem to be just another white cloud in the sky. So the fast-diving gull gets a meal.

Scientists once invented an illusion that tricked a kitten. They painted part of a tabletop to look as if it had a checkered cloth on it. Then they painted the rest of the table to make it look as if the cloth was hanging straight down over the edge. The kitten walked across the painted "cloth," but when it came to the phony edge, it stopped and would not go on. Its eyes saw a cliff instead of a flat tabletop.

The same kind of illusion gives people a lot of laughs at fun houses in amusement parks.

ZANY BUT BRAINY

Mathematicians of a very special kind have some strange and wonderful ideas about shapes. The math they study is called topology, and they are topologists. Their ideas are serious, but you can have a lot of fun with them, too.

PRETZEL BENDER

s a pretzel the same as a Halloween mask? Topologists' answer is yes, and they aren't joking! They say that two things are alike if you can bend and stretch one of them into the shape of the other. You can poke and shove as much as you like, but you must not make any extra holes or pinch any holes shut. Of course, you have to transform your pretzel while it is still soft dough. So topologists pretend that everything is made of stretchable putty.

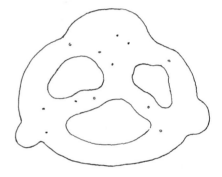

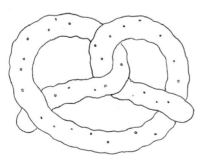

MATH YOU CAN EAT

Here is a soft pretzel recipe for doing topological experiments.

1 $\frac{1}{2}$ cups warm water

1 envelope yeast

1 tablespoon sugar

4 cups flour

coarse salt

sesame seeds

Mix the first three ingredients. Add flour and knead. Flour your hands if the dough is too sticky at first. It will become stretchable as you work with it.

After experimenting, twist into pretzel shapes, sprinkle salt or seeds on the pretzels, and let rise for thirty minutes. Bake thirty minutes at 350 degrees.

Suppose you start your next topological problem with a baseball made of dough. What can you turn it into?

Can you find two things that you can transform a doughnut into?

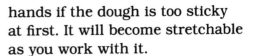

WOODCHUCK CATCHING

Mr. Chen doesn't know anything about topology, but he does like to protect wild animals. One day he heard that a work crew was going to bulldoze a Colorado field where a woodchuck has its den. If he could catch the woodchuck in a special trap, he could take it to a safe new home.

Suppose Mr. Chen asks you to help. First, you and he have to bait the trap with paintbrush flowers. Paintbrush is a western woodchuck's favorite food. Just to be sure it finds the food, you and Mr. Chen make a long, snaky path, with wire fencing on each side, all the way from the woodchuck's den to the trap at the end.

You and Mr. Chen set up the fence, winding it in a spiral around the den. "That will get the little fellow," says Mr. Chen.

Do you think he is right? Use your finger to trace the path the woodchuck will have to take. Are you surprised?

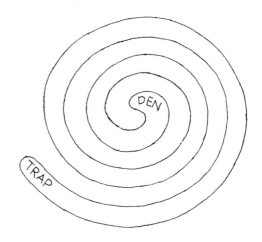

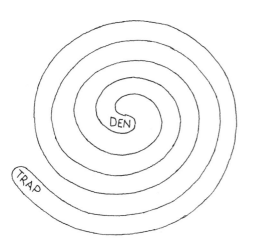

Now suppose you and Mr. Chen had started the winding path a little differently. You could have made the loops round the den the way you see it in the second picture. Trace this one with your finger. Are you surprised again?

Take another look at the picture of the two ways Mr. Chen could make the path to the woodchuck trap. Hold a straightedge across the first one from the den to the field outside. Now you can use math to find out whether the trap at the end of the fence would catch the woodchuck. All you have to do is count the number of times the straightedge crosses the fence. It crosses six times. Six is an even number, and the woodchuck escapes.

The second picture looks almost exactly the same, but the loop starts differently, and the straightedge crosses the fence seven times. That's an odd number. And you and Mr. Chen trap the woodchuck.

THE SECRET RULE

Here are three simple diagrams that show the secret of the odd-even rule.

Did you think that the picture of the woodchuck trap was just an ordinary spiral? Look again. It was really a circular shape that has been stretched. That is why topologists are intrigued by it. Their name for it is the Norton Curve because the first person who experimented with it was Camille Norton.

Of course, topologists don't stop at anything this simple. The squiggly diagram below is one of their problems: Is the place marked with a star inside or outside the Norton Curve, which begins at the place marked with a C? You can use the odd-even test to find out.

Question: Why does the king of Spain always have holes in his pants?

Answer: Simple. How else could he get into them?

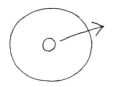

Crosses 1 line, can't get out

Crosses 2 lines, can get out

Crosses 3 lines, can't get out

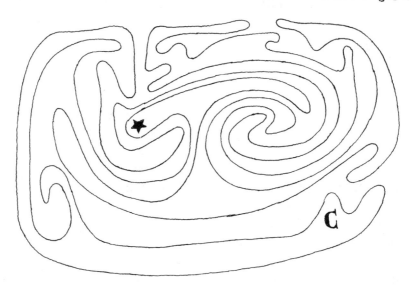

PIPLIP

Meet Piplip. He is the brainchild of a topologist. Piplip has one problem. He gets sick if he eats anything that is not exactly like him topologically. He knows this, and that's why he had a tantrum in the supermarket one day.

Piplip's mother had taken a package from the dairy counter and said, "We'll have this for lunch."

"I won't eat that," Piplip screamed. "It will kill me!"

"Calm down," said his mother. "Don't worry. I'm going to fix it so it won't make you sick."

What did Piplip's mother plan to do?

Look back at the picture of Piplip and you will see he has seven corners and four holes. His mother sliced a piece of Swiss cheese so that it had not only four holes but seven corners—the perfect topological lunch.

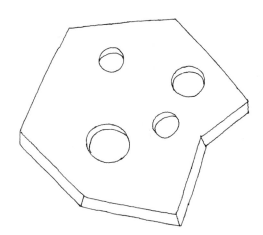

PREDICTIONS

Topologists are interested in predictions. (No, they don't do horoscopes.) Suppose you begin one of their problems like this:

Take a piece of string, cut it, and lay it on the table. You will have two pieces. Now fold a longer piece of string into a simple U shape. If you cut it straight across, how many pieces will you have? Three.

Take a longer piece, fold it as you did the first time, and then bring the ends around to make another fold. Cut across it, and you will have five pieces.

With a third string, much longer, make three folds, and cut across. This time you get nine pieces.

You could go on with longer and longer pieces of string and more folds, but this is enough to show you what interests topologists. They can predict the answer you will get every time from now on with every added fold and cut, no matter how long you go on with the experiment.

This is the number sequence: 0 pieces, 1 piece, 2 pieces, 3 pieces, 5 pieces, 9 pieces. Do you see something special here? Topologists see a pattern. First you have no pieces, then $0 + 1$, then $1 + 1$, then $2 + 1$, then $4 + 1$, then $8 + 1$.

How can you predict your next cut? The pattern shows that before each cut you multiply by two the number resulting from the previous cut and add 1. So your answer is $8 \times 2 + 1 = 17$ pieces.

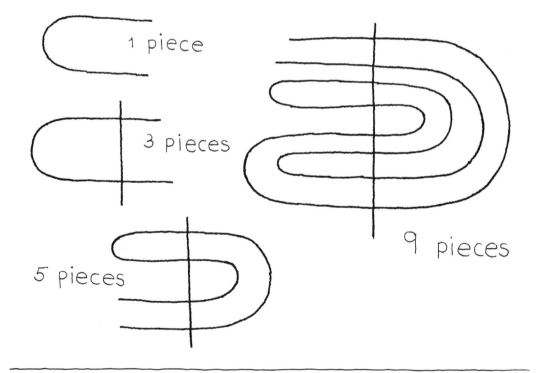

1 piece

3 pieces

5 pieces

9 pieces

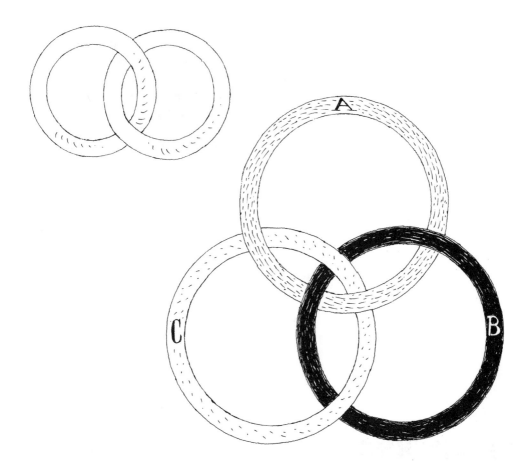

THREE-RING CIRCUS

Look at the drawing of two rings linked together. There is no doubt that they won't come apart unless you cut one of them.

Look at the second drawing. All three seem to be linked. But are they? A topologist would tell you to look at them one by one.

Paying no attention to the ring labeled C, follow Ring A around, and you'll see that it crosses *below* Ring B and is not linked to it.

Now follow Ring A around to the places where it crosses Ring C, paying no attention this time to Ring B. Ring A passes *above* Ring C. No linking here.

Next, see where B crosses A and where B crosses C. Again you see no linking.

Finally, see where C crosses B and where it crosses A. No link!

The more you look at the rings the more puzzling—even annoying—they are. But they interest a topologist, because they belong to the knot family, and there is a branch of topology called *knot theory*.

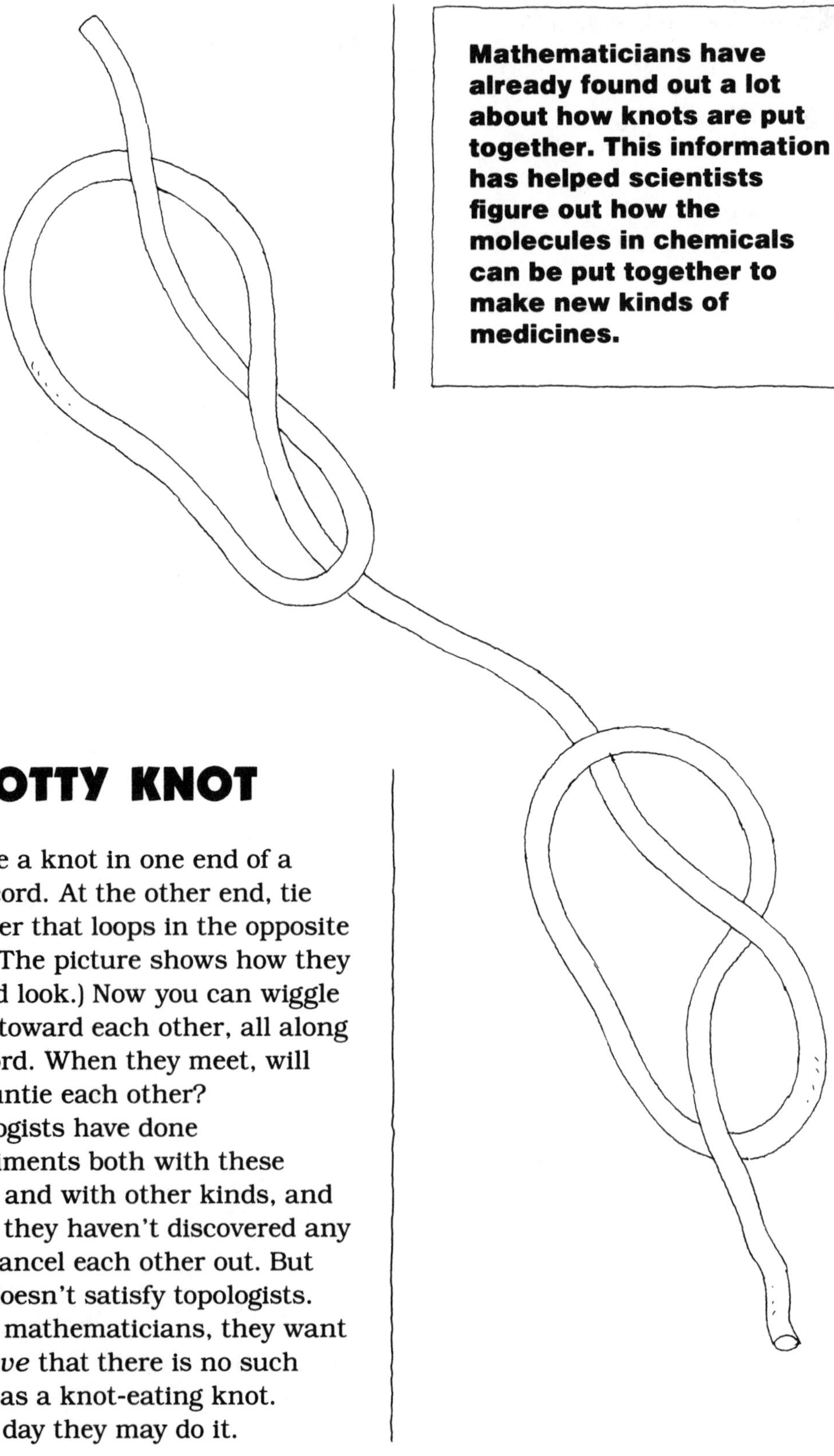

Mathematicians have already found out a lot about how knots are put together. This information has helped scientists figure out how the molecules in chemicals can be put together to make new kinds of medicines.

KNOTTY KNOT

Tie a knot in one end of a cord. At the other end, tie another that loops in the opposite way. (The picture shows how they should look.) Now you can wiggle them toward each other, all along the cord. When they meet, will they untie each other? Topologists have done experiments both with these knots and with other kinds, and so far they haven't discovered any that cancel each other out. But that doesn't satisfy topologists. Being mathematicians, they want to *prove* that there is no such thing as a knot-eating knot. Some day they may do it.

FREAKY FIGURE

Can you imagine something that has only one side? Suppose you cut a long, narrow strip of paper and join the two ends together to form a band. You can run your finger around the inside, but you have to lift your finger to touch the outside. No doubt about it, a band of paper has to have two sides.

That is what everybody thought until one day a mathematician made an astonishing object that had only one side. His name was Augustus Möbius (pronounced MO-bee-us), and his famous invention is called the Möbius strip.

It's easy to make one of these amazing objects. Just cut a long, narrow strip of paper, draw an X on both sides, give it a twist, and then join the ends together with tape or paste. This, too, is a band. Now test it by running your finger over its surface. Your finger will pass over one X, go on around, and then pass over the other X without being lifted. What was once an inside and an outside has become one continuous side. It was the twist in the strip that did the trick.

Topologists have done a lot of experiments with Möbius strips and have had fun with them, too. Here is one of their stunts:

Cut a strip, but before making a band, write on one side:

It was a dark and stormy night. We were all seated around the room

Turn the strip over (flip it; don't turn it end to end), and write:

when someone said, "Captain, tell us a story," and the captain said

Be sure to write the words in exactly the position shown in the diagram. Twist the strip, and paste the tab marked B2 on top of A1.

Now you will have two remarkable things to show your friends: an object with only one side and a story that never ends.

TRICKY BELT

Can you think of a practical use for this strange Möbius strip? When it is made into a belt to run machinery in a factory, it lasts much longer than an ordinary belt. An ordinary one has two sides, one of which is constantly rubbed as it passes over rollers. After a while the rubbing makes the belt too rough to run smoothly. The twist in the Möbius belt forces not just half but every part of it to be rubbed on the rollers. Therefore, it does not wear out nearly so fast.

A1 | It was a dark and stormy night. We were all seated around the room | A2

B1 | when someone said, "Captain, tell us a story," and the captain said | B2

the captain said | B2 | A1 | It was a

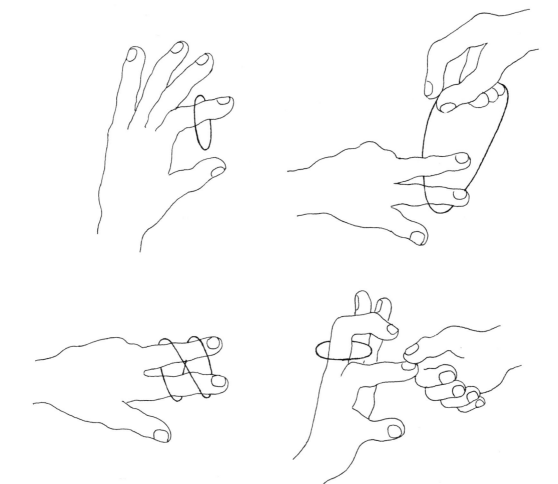

KNOT-AND-LOOP ACT

By now, topologists have shown you enough tricks to entertain friends and grown-ups and even first-graders. Show off with a knot-and-loop act.

Loop a rubber band around your first finger, then back and under your middle finger, and finally put it around your first finger again. Be sure to follow *exactly* what the sketches show. Ask someone to hold the tip of your first finger. This will prove that you aren't doing anything phony with the loop. As your helper pulls on your first finger, curl up your middle finger. The band will leap away and end up hanging from the middle finger. This works best with a thin rubber band that allows the middle finger to bend easily.

INDEX